Wild America

A personal celebration of the National Parks

David Muench & Roly Smith

Wild America

Published simultaneously in the US and UK, 2016

Rucksack Readers, 6 Old Church Lane, Edinburgh, EH15 3PX, UK
www.rucsacs.com

Rucksack Readers USA, Interlink Publishing, 46 Crosby Street,
Northampton, Massachusetts 01060, USA
www.interlinkbooks.com

ISBN 978-1-898481-73-7

British Library cataloguing in publication data: a catalogue
record for this book is available from the British Library

Library of Congress Cataloging-in-Publication Data available

Designed in the UK by Ian Clydesdale *www.workhorse.co.uk*

Printed and bound in China by Hong Kong Graphics & Printing
using non-chemical soya-based inks, on acid-free paper from
sustainable forests.

Front cover: Mt Tyndal, Sequoia National Park
Title page: Agua Canyon, Bryce Canyon
Back cover: Sandstone slabs, Zion National Park

Contents

National Parks

Other protected areas

America's best idea

Thousands of tired, nerve-shaken, over-civilized people are beginning to find out that going to the mountains is going home; that wildness is a necessity; and mountain parks and reservations are useful not only as fountains of timber and irrigating rivers, but as fountains of life.

John Muir, *Our National Parks* (1901)

Americans are justly proud of their national parks, often dubbed the best idea that this emerging nation gave to the rest of the world. Even if you can't get out to experience them first-hand, the mere fact that the gushing geysers of Yellowstone, the bristling pinnacles of Bryce and Zion and the wild Atlantic coast of Acadia exist is still a source of intense national pride.

This rich natural heritage, as preserved in its wonderful national parks system, performs the same function in the national identity, culture and psyche of the US as do the castles, cathedrals, and ancient cities for the nations of the Old World.

When national parks were first being proposed in America in the mid-19th century, Clarence King, later first director of the US Geological Survey, explored the gigantic Sierra redwoods of King's Canyon. In his classic *Mountaineering in the Sierra Nevada* (1872) King rejected the common idea that culture should derive solely from man-made artefacts. He suggested that: '…no fragment of human work, broken pillar or sand-worn image … link to the past and to-day with anything like the power of these monuments of living antiquity…'.

Horace Greeley, editor of the New York Tribune wrote in 1859 that America's past must be measured in 'green old age' and by 'earth monuments' like the Sierra redwoods, which had stood before the birth of Christ. No longer, argued King and Greeley, need the citizens of the New World live in the shadow of the feudal legacy of Europe's castles and cathedrals; they had their own living heritage of natural beauty.

And if there was one moment when the notion of national parks and the preservation of scenery became ingrained into the American consciousness, it was in 1903 when President Theodore Roosevelt took time out from his political duties to spend a three-night camping trip with John Muir, the Scots-born 'father' of US national parks, among the granite spires and sequoia groves of Yosemite. At the time, Yosemite was a Californian State Park, signed off by President Abraham Lincoln in the depths of the Civil War in 1864.

Evidently it was a meeting of minds, and Roosevelt became one of the strongest proponents of the national parks idea, creating five new ones – including Yosemite three years after his memorable visit – and more than 200 other protected areas during his eight-year term of office.

Whose idea was it?

An insignificant 7549-foot pine-covered peak at the confluence of the Firehole and Gibbon Rivers in Yellowstone National Park, Montana, bears the notable name of 'National Park Mountain.'

This unusual appellation came about because it was apparently around a campfire in its shadow in September 1870 that Cornelius Hedges, a young Helena lawyer and newspaper correspondent, first suggested that Yellowstone should be made a national park.

Hedges was a member of the Washburn-Doane expedition which had been charged with surveying the Yellowstone area and reporting back on some of the unbelievable stories which had been filtering through about the region. Grizzled mountain men like Jim Bridger and John Colter had come back with extraordinary tales of boiling rivers, hot springs and geysers. But they were simply not believed.

As they sat around that campfire that chilly September night, the expedition members earnestly discussed how the obvious real estate and mineral resources of the area could best be exploited. But Hedges begged to disagree. There should be no private ownership of the Yellowstone, he said. It should be a great national park for all people to enjoy for ever.

Hedges' words evidently struck a chord with the other members of the expedition, who had been awed by the 'unlimited grandeur and beauty' that bore out everything the old trappers had reported. Particularly affected was Nathaniel Langford, a local businessman, who immediately started a vigorous campaign to realize the dream. Two years later, in 1872 Yellowstone became the world's first national park when it was 'dedicated and set apart as a public park or pleasuring ground for the benefit and enjoyment of the people.'

Dawn on the Yellowstone River, Yellowstone National Park

Fall palette, Mt Moran, Grand Teton National Park

Although the campfire story may be apocryphal, it is often cited as the birth of the American and, by association, of the global national park movement. It was certainly not the first mention of the idea. The great artist-recorder of Native American life, George Catlin, had come up with something very similar nearly 40 years before.

In a letter to the *New York Daily Commercial Advertiser*, written in 1832 while he was camping at the mouth of the Teton River, he recommended the creation of a 'nation's park' for the great herds of bison which then roamed the northern plains at the confluence of the Yellowstone River with the Upper Missouri, for the Indians and their wild homeland.

'What a beautiful and thrilling specimen for America to preserve and hold up to the view of her refined citizens and the world, in future ages!' Catlin enthused. 'A nation's park containing man and beast, in all the wild freshness of nature's beauty.'

Unfortunately, Catlin's inclusive vision for parks didn't sway the politicians, and while the parks were dedicated to preservation, many of the native people who had preserved them for countless generations were evicted when they were set up, as were the hillbillies of Shenandoah National Park 60 years later.

Over 20 years before, the celebrated English Romantic poet William Wordsworth may have been the first to put the national park idea into words. In the concluding paragraphs of his *Guide through the District of the Lakes in the North of England* of 1810, he expressed the hope that landowners would join him in his wish 'to preserve the native beauty of this delightful district'. He famously suggested his beloved Lake District might be: '…a sort of national property, in which every man has a right and interest who has an eye to perceive and a heart to enjoy'.

A 'Magna Carta' for the parks

Whoever first came up with the idea, it was the United States that made it a reality. America's national parks became the blueprint for national parks now found in around 100 countries throughout the world. And the US National Park Service, whose centenary we celebrate in this book, became the model which many other countries have adopted.

The chief proponent of the NPS was J Horace McFarland, a Pennsylvania printer, publisher and horticulturalist. As first president of the American Civic Association, it was his campaign against a proposal to harness the Niagara River for hydro-electric power which first galvanized him into action.

The earliest parks were being run by a mixture of the Forest Service, the Interior Department and even, in the case of Yosemite and Sequoia, the US Cavalry's all-black 'Buffalo Soldiers'. Eventually, after continued pressure by people like McFarland and architect Frederick Law Olmsted Jr, a draft bill to create a 'Bureau of National Parks' was first presented to Congress in 1910. But it was lost in political filibustering over the next five years.

After a summer vacation in the High Sierra in 1914, self-made borax millionaire and Sierra Club member Stephen T Mather had been angered by what he saw as the poor management of Yosemite National Park. Mather immediately fired off a letter of protest to Interior Secretary, Franklin K Lane. Lane's reply famously came back: 'Dear Steve: If you don't like the way the national parks are being run, come on down to Washington and run them yourself'.

Lane's invitation sealed the success of the emerging National Park Service. Mather took up the challenge while insisting that his friend, the energetic young lawyer Horace M Albright (who was to become his eventual successor), should join him as his assistant, to protect him from the inevitable bureaucracy and red tape. Between them, they were to guide the pioneering work and shape the future of the NPS for the next 20 years.

The National Park Service 'Organic' Act, as drafted by Olmsted, was finally signed by President Woodrow Wilson on August 25, 1916. The purpose of this 'Magna Carta' for national parks was: 'to conserve the scenery and the natural and historic objects and the wild life therein and to provide for the enjoyment of the same in such manner and by such means as will leave them unimpaired for the enjoyment of future generations'.

There are now 59 designated national parks in 27 states of America from Alaska to Florida – the latest being the volcanic monoliths of The Pinnacles in California's Coast Range, designated in 2013. And the 20,000-strong National Park Service now administers nearly 400 protected sites throughout the country, which are visited by more than 275 million people annually.

Piñon cones and daisies, Mesa Verde National Park

Wild America

I've been lucky enough to explore many of America's finest national parks and protected sites over the last 20 years. I've greeted the first rays of the sun to reach the country from the bald granite summit of Cadillac Mountain in Acadia National Park, and watched the sun set over the boundless Pacific from the rocky Oregon coast. I've been left speechless by the unfathomable depths of the Grand Canyon, the indescribable blueness of Crater Lake and the soaring granite spires of Yosemite. I've also gazed at the myriad of stars from the midnight depths of Bryce Canyon.

But David Muench, my distinguished partner in this book, has far more experience of America's wildernesses than I'll ever have. He's been photographing them for over 50 years and is rightly recognized as the doyen of US wilderness photography. As he has written: 'Sacred and spiritual, the national parks, with their primal beauty, have focused and transformed my vision into a sense of reality, a kind of super realism that reveals the vital essence of wildness in the American landscape'.

Our personal selection of 21 national parks and protected areas does not set out to be a comprehensive guide to the wildest places in America, otherwise it would have included places such as Alaska and Hawaii. We share our title with a 1956 transatlantic partnership between American wildlife illustrator Roger Tory Peterson and British naturalist James Fisher. Like their book, our *Wild America* is a personal celebration of places we have visited and of our experiences in them. We apologize in advance if you find some of your favorite places missing. In our defense, both David and I had to leave out many of our own.

Perhaps the last word, as the first, should be left with the parks' founding father, John Muir, describing 'Our National Parks':

Climb the mountains and get their good tidings. Nature's peace will flow into you as sunshine flows into trees. The winds will blow their own freshness into you, and the storms their energy, while cares will drop off like autumn leaves.

Upper and Lower Yosemite Falls, Yosemite National Park

8

*'I stood upon the hills, when heaven's wide arch
Was glorious with the sun's returning march'*

Henry Wadsworth Longfellow, 1839

Frenchman Bay from the summit of Cadillac Mountain

Dawning of America

If you get up early enough, from the smooth granite 1530-ft summit of Cadillac Mountain in Acadia National Park you'll be among the first to see dawn in the United States. You'll catch the first warm rays of the sun spreading over the prickly tree-topped summits of the Porcupine Islands in Frenchman Bay, with the vast expanse of Atlantic beyond reflecting the rising golden orb.

The best approach to Acadia's reigning summit is the North Ridge Trail from near where the Park Loop Road becomes one-way. This 2½ mile, signposted trail offers the best views of Bar Harbor and Frenchman Bay, and you'll bask in a far greater sense of achievement than the masses who have taken the switchback, 3½-mile mountain road from the Visitor Center, then a short walk to the summit.

The bare summit – the highest on the eastern coastline of the Americas north of Rio de Janeiro – is decorated by wind-blasted, pygmy *krummholz* junipers and pines, and the 360° view is unsurpassed in Acadia.

In the mid-19th century Mt Desert Island, which forms the major part of the park, was a fashionable resort for the so-called 'summer people' of New England. Acadia National Park was established in 1919 after 40 years of tireless campaigning by wealthy summer residents like George B Dorr and John D Rockefeller Jr, who lived in enormous, 80-room mansions which they knew as 'cottages', and were called 'rusticators' for their love of the rural life.

It was a highly convoluted story. George Dorr negotiated his way through a minefield of land speculation, calling-in of favors, political intrigue and the wielding of power

Fall in Acadia

The Bubbles from Jordan Pond

and influence to create Acadia National Park. Known as 'the father of Acadia', Dorr stated in his *Story of Acadia National Park* (1942): 'Whatever changes come, the Park as a possession of the people will be as permanent, doubtless, as man's need for recreation and enjoyment of great coastal scenery.'

Acadia is famed for its 57-mile network of traffic-free carriage roads constructed through the forest, and over 17 handsome granite bridges by oil magnate Rockefeller between 1910 and 1940. Rockefeller moved to his 150-acre estate in 1910, just as a row was brewing over the ban on the use of motorized vehicles on Mt Desert Island.

He conceived the idea of building a series of gravel roads on his property where he could enjoy the pleasure of horse-drawn carriage rides. Eventually, the network spread to other estates, including the Park Loop Road and an access road to the popular destination of Jordan Pond, watched over by the twin glacially-rounded summits of The Bubbles.

To get some idea of Rockefeller's vision, we and a group of jolly retired farmers from Ohio enjoyed a delightful six-mile, two-hour carriage ride (drawn by two handsome Suffolk Punches, Finn and Furb) from the Wildwood Stables in the heart of the park.

The route took us past Long Pond and the site of Rockfeller's mansion at Barr Hill, crossing the magnificent Cobblestone Bridge over Jordan Stream, the elegant, three-arched Duck Brook Bridge, and Deer Brook Bridge, with circular stone medallions dating its construction to 1925.

Rockefeller is said to have claimed that these bridges might as well have well been built of diamonds for what they cost him. But he could afford it, for by the time he died in 1937 he was the richest man in the world.

Mt Desert Island is considered to be one of America's premier birding locations, and James Audubon, inspiration for the National Audubon Society, did much of his early research here. I was taken on a birdwatching walk with naturalist Rich MacDonald of Bar Harbor's National History Center, from Sieur de Monts Spring in the shadow of the mountain named for George Dorr.

With Rich's expert help, we spotted 13 species, including black-capped chickadees, hermit thrushes, a dark-eyed junco, a red-breasted nuthatch, and a beautiful gold-crowned kinglet on our walk through the forest. We also caught the tail flash of a shy, white-tailed deer disappearing into the undergrowth.

To crown our visit to Acadia, we dined in the spectacular dining room of the Looking Glass Restaurant on the hills overlooking Bar Harbor. We were rewarded by the stunning sight of a bright orange 'supermoon' rising where we had seen the sun rise that morning, reflected in the still, island-studded waters of Frenchman Bay.

We felt we'd found our Arcadia in Acadia.

Bass Harbor Lighthouse

Antelope Canyon Navajo Tribal Park

*The red, pink and orange
sandstone rocks swirled and
flowed around us in fantastic
scalloped and surreal patterns …*

Antelope Canyon

13

Desert dessert

It was like walking through an enormous whipped-cream dessert. The red, pink and orange sandstone rocks swirled and flowed around us in fantastic, scalloped and surreal patterns, lit by occasional shafts of sunlight which filtered down, placing dramatic spotlights on the flat, sandy floor.

We were exploring the Upper Antelope Canyon, near Page, Arizona, one of the most famous and most photographed slot canyons in the world. A sense of almost religious, jaw-dropping awe overtook our party as we wandered through the 600-foot-long, winding trail, with the walls towering 120 feet above us.

The skies had begun to cloud over as we reached the top of the canyon and started to retrace our steps. We were close to the entrance when a few photographers noticed spots of rain splashing their lenses. 'Come on,' said our knowledgeable Navajo guide, a sense of urgency suddenly entering her voice: 'we need to get out of here – and quick!'.

Before we knew it, waterfalls of chocolate brown water were cascading down the walls of the canyon, and floodwater was gushing down the floor and spreading out of the canyon mouth. We turned and ran for the entrance, realizing that we were witnessing at first hand one of the famous, deadly flash floods which are such a major hazard of these deceptively beautiful slot canyons.

Our guide had warned us that rain does not have to fall on or near these canyons for floods to surge through them. Downpours dozens of miles away upstream can funnel through them without notice. Earlier that year, several tourists had been stranded on a ledge when two flash floods similar to the one we had witnessed occurred in Upper Antelope Canyon. Some were rescued and others just had to wait for the flood waters to recede.

And only 13 years before, 11 tourists had been killed in the more dangerous Lower Antelope Canyon by another flash flood. Little rain had fallen on that day, but an earlier thunderstorm had dumped a large amount of water in the canyon basin, seven miles upstream. And in 2006, a flash flood had lasted for 36 hours and caused the Tribal Park authorities to close Lower Antelope Canyon for a period of five months.

As we bumped our way in our SUV across the arroyo back to Page, we realized with gratitude why Antelope Canyon must always be visited on a guided Navajo tour. And we appreciated the accuracy of the Navajo name for Upper Antelope Canyon – *Tse' bighanilini* – 'the place where water runs through rocks'.

It was water, of course, that created these masterpieces of Nature. They were formed by floods eroding the soft Navajo Sandstone, especially during the so-called summer 'desert monsoon' season. Picking up speed and abrasive sand grains as they surge through the narrow slots, they carve them ever deeper, smoothing away the hard edges like a natural sandpaper and creating the characteristic flowing shapes in the rock that we admire today.

The English name of Antelope Canyon (it is also sometimes known as Corkscrew Canyon) comes from the time when prong-horned antelopes pranced through it, but the only animals we saw on our visit were other camera-clicking humans.

The Navajo name for Lower Antelope Canyon, a couple of miles away, is *Hasdeztwazi*, which is equally descriptive and means 'spiral rock arches.' Prior to the installation of metal stairways, visiting the Lower Canyon required climbing wooden ladders, and it remains a much more difficult proposition than the Upper Canyon. It is longer, much shallower and narrower, and requires some climbing and sturdy footwear. Lower Antelope Canyon still attracts a number of determined photographers, although casual sightseers are much less common than in the Upper Canyon.

Our guide explained that to the Navajo people, entering Antelope Canyon was like entering a cathedral. 'We pause before entering to be in the right frame of mind and as a sign of respect' she said. 'This also allows us to leave feeling uplifted by Nature, and to be in harmony with something greater than ourselves. It is a spiritual experience.' We said amen to that.

To the Navajo people, entering Antelope Canyon was like entering a cathedral.

'The finest quality of this…desert landscape is the indifference manifest to our presence …'

Edward Abbey

Klondike Bluffs framed by Tower Arch

15

Abbey's road

In the mid-1950s, Edward Abbey, author and outspoken environmentalist, served for two years as a summer seasonal ranger at Arches National Monument (now a national park). He lived in a trailer provided for him by the Park Service.

He recorded his experiences in his classic *Desert Solitare* (1968), in which he communicated his passionate love of Utah's red rock desert country, and his fears for its future. It is as much a polemic against development and excessive tourism in the national parks as it is a wonderful piece of nature writing, which some have compared to Thoreau's *Walden* and Leopold's *A Sand County Almanac.*

Inspired by Abbey's enthusiasm I first came to Arches National Park and found, as expected, that many of his forecasts had come to pass. There were metalled roads where in his day there were dirt tracks. There were car parks and pit toilets, and a large, low-rise visitor center had been built at the southern entrance. And a well-appointed campground had sprung up at the once remote Devil's Garden trailhead in the far north of the park.

Many have condemned Abbey's attitude to the urbanization of the parks as elitist. On his criteria, many thousands of less-mobile visitors would not be able to enjoy the glories of this and many other wonderful wilderness areas.

As I joined the throng gathered round the duty ranger at the Balanced Rock pull-out (parking layby), I asked myself just who are national parks for? And I concluded they weren't set aside just for fit, active and experienced outdoors people: they were reserved for their priceless wildlife, and later for everyone to enjoy. So I didn't mind joining the crocodile of people

Turret Arch

Landscape Arch

taking the three-mile round trail to perhaps the most iconic feature of the park – the improbable giant's croquet hoop of Delicate Arch.

We set off from Civil War veteran John Wesley Wolfe's log Bar-DX farmstead, where he had lived for 20 years from 1888. Behind the ranch under an overhanging alcove in the sandstone, I found the Ute petroglyphs of a hunting scene of mounted warriors chasing bighorn

sheep, which I'd discovered on a previous visit. It must have been etched around 200 years ago, because the Utes did not acquire horses until the early 1800s.

The trail rose over slick rock and through dusty arroyos until it reached the final climb up to a 200-yard rock terrace, slanting towards our hidden goal. The first window in the rocks appeared high up the slick rock to our left, and I couldn't resist the scramble up to get the first view of Delicate Arch, neatly framed in this natural aperture.

Delicate Arch is truly a wonder of nature, its 65-foot high hoop framing a distant view of the snow-topped La Sal Mountains. We scrambled down into the sweeping amphitheater at its foot and later up to the canyon opposite to get different views of this famous landmark, which is now depicted on Utah license plates.

Arches is an extraordinary place for natural arches. It's claimed there are as many as 2000 of these freaks of differential erosion carved in the soft Entrada sandstone of the Colorado Plateau. There seem to be arches everywhere you look, including the North and South Windows and the Double and Turret Arches in the Windows Section of the park.

Perhaps the most rewarding are the wispy sweep of Landscape Arch stretching across the desert sky, Tunnel Arch and Double O Arch, all to be found beyond the Devil's Garden trailhead.

The entrance and exit to Arches National Park is equally dramatic, passing the monolithic red rock guardians of the Courthouse Towers, Park Avenue, the Three Gossips, the Tower of Babel and The Organ. Having been lucky enough to experience this precious yet fragile wilderness, it seems appropriate to leave the last word to Edward Abbey for those who could not:

A man could be a lover and defender of the wilderness without ever in his lifetime leaving the boundaries of asphalt, power lines, and right-angled surfaces. We need wilderness whether or not we ever set foot in it. We need a refuge even though we may never need to go there.

Storm approaching Delicate Arch

Badlands National Park

'I've been about the world a lot and pretty much over our own country, but I was totally unprepared for that revelation called the Dakota Bad Lands.'

Frank Lloyd Wright

Twin Peaks, Cedar Pass

The desert blooms

The ranger at the Ben Reifel Visitor Center at the Cedar Pass entrance to Badlands National Park was enthusiastic. 'You're going to see the park at its very best' he predicted. Badlands receives only 16 inches of rain a year, but recent heavy rains had turned the park green, and its normally arid landscape was bursting into bloom.

The surrounding 170,000 acres of rolling protected prairies were transformed from their usual summer biscuit-brown to a lush green, where wildflowers such as purple thistles, magenta spiderworts, scarlet gayfeathers, golden prairie cones and sunflowers grabbed their brief chance to reach for the sun.

I really didn't know what to expect from the Badlands – a term commonly used for barren, severely-eroded landscapes from Montana to Mongolia. The Oglala Lakota Sioux named it *mako sica*, which means the same thing. But, as architect Frank Lloyd Wright had discovered 70 years before, it was a revelation.

We took the Badlands Loop Road towards Bigfoot Pass, and it was like driving through a miniature version of the Grand Canyon. The serried colors of the towers, spires and ridges of severely eroded Chadron and Brule sedimentary rocks dating from the Eocene epoch (about 55 million years ago) were as Lloyd Wright had described them: 'a distant architecture, ethereal … an endless supernatural world more spiritual than earth but created out of it'.

The 30-mile Badlands Loop Road was constructed in the 1930s at the instigation of US Senator Peter Norbeck and his friend Ben Millard. They were tireless campaigners in the 25-year campaign to make the Badlands a national park.

Clay spires, Badlands

As we reached the Saddle Pass pull-out, the lure of the hills overcame me. I set off up the steep trail through the ghostly-white hoodoos (rock pinnacles) and spires to Saddle Pass, and its junction with the Castle and Medicine Root Trails. It was a little disconcerting as I set off to see several signs warning of rattlesnakes, and I enquired nervously of fellow walkers returning down the trail if they had seen any. They hadn't, and thankfully I didn't come across any either, but I made my progress as noisy as possible.

The view from the top of the trail was extensive, taking in the vast expanse of the 48,000-acre Buffalo Gap National Grassland, now glowing green after the recent rain. This was where the previously extinct black-footed ferret had been successfully reintroduced in 1994.

Descending from Bigfoot Pass and passing Panorama Point, we entered the 64,000-acre Badlands Wilderness Area at Dillon Pass. Here the distinctive Yellow Mounds, deposited on the floor of the Pierre Sea during the Cretaceous era 70 million years ago, had been stained by iron oxides to give them their vivid color.

Three miles further on, we found the aptly named Pinnacles Overlook. A silent city of concrete-gray rock pinnacles rose from an emerald green forest of junipers.

After the Pinnacles entrance, we took the 40-mile unpaved Sage Creek Rim Road, which climbed up onto the plateau with extensive views south across the Badlands Wilderness Area. We soon came across the Roberts Prairie Dog Town where, despite their barking warning, we watched as several of these inquisitive little rodents were dive-bombed by two marauding ravens.

We also saw some of the Badlands' 1000-strong herd of reintroduced bison grazing peacefully in the

Storm clouds over Badlands Wilderness Area

21

distance, but a couple of miles further on along the dirt road, we had a close encounter with two huge, shaggy bulls.

An erratic line of posts lined the road. The bulls were obviously being irritated by their moulting hides. We watched, fascinated, as they revelled in the scratching posts, a look of sheer ecstasy lighting up their massive horned and bearded heads.

Like so much of the American prairies, when the Badlands were first designated as a national monument in 1939 there were no bison left. Deliberate over-predation by humans had, in a matter of decades, reduced the population from perhaps 40-50 million animals to a few hundred scattered survivors. So it was heartening to see, as we left The Badlands, the return of these magnificent natives.

Sunset at Cedar Pass

Black Canyon of the Gunnison National Park

'We entered a gorge, remote from the sun, where the rocks were two thousand feet sheer and where a rock-splintered river roared and howled.'

Rudyard Kipling, 1889

The Gunnison River from the North Rim of the canyon

River deep, mountain high

The Black Canyon of the Gunnison is one of the youngest of America's national parks but paradoxically it has some of the oldest rocks. It was made a national park by President Bill Clinton only in 1999, but the Precambrian gneiss and schists that make up its forbidding walls were formed some 1.7 billion years ago, making them some of the oldest rocks on earth.

The canyon's name comes from Captain John Gunnison, who made a tough crossing of the Lake Fork of the river named after him in September 1853, bypassing it to head west to the Uncompahgre.

The 'black' comes from the canyon's extreme depth and the fact that it is usually in dark shadow. In fact, some parts of the gorge receive only half an hour of sunlight every day and at its narrowest point, the canyon is only 40 feet wide. As Duane Vandenbusche wrote in 2009: 'Several canyons of the American West are longer and some are deeper, but none combines the depth, sheerness, narrowness, darkness and dread of the Black Canyon'.

When seen from the Painted Wall viewpoint on the south rim, the magnificent wall opposite, marbled with the weaving pink streamers of pegmatite intrusions across its dark surface, is 2240 feet above the river – nearly twice the height of the Empire State Building.

The truly awe-inspiring sight includes a vertiginous glimpse of the green waters of the boiling river far below. White-throated swifts flash by over the stunted Gambel oak and serviceberry scrub, which somehow manage to survive nearly 8000 feet above sea level.

The awesome gorge of the canyon

Western Colorado is famous for its spectacular sunsets, and on a clear day those from Sunset View on the South Rim are particularly impressive. Looking downstream, the view extends for 30 miles over the vast, 500-square-mile expanse of the Grand Mesa plateau – at 10,000-feet it has a claim to be the world's largest flat-topped mountain.

During the Gunnison Uplift of about 60 million years ago, the Gunnison River cut down like a knife through butter to create the awesome gorge of the Black Canyon. The river still drops an average of 34 feet per mile throughout the entire 48-mile canyon, making it the fifth steepest in North America. In comparison, the Colorado River only drops an average of 7½ feet per mile through the Grand Canyon.

In the two miles between Pulpit Rock and Chasm View, the Gunnison drops an astonishing 480 feet over a maelstrom of rapids, chutes and waterfalls. But the river takes its time. Over the last two million years, it has been carving out the chasm at the rate of an inch per century – the same rate of growth as a human hair.

One of the first explorations of the inner depths of the Black Canyon was made in 1882, when General William Jackson Palmer sent his engineer Bryan Bryant to survey a possible route for his narrow-gauge Denver & Rio Grande Western Railroad through it.

Bryant set off with a 12-man team, confidently expecting to complete the survey in 20 days. When he returned, bruised and battered, 68 days later, he

Summer storm clouds gather above the Grand Mesa

25

reported to Palmer: 'Eight of the 12-man crew left after a few days, terrified of the task in front of them. What the rest of the men saw was spectacular and had never been seen by another human.'

Bryant concluded that it was impossible to build a railroad through the depths of the canyon, and estimated that the cost might be up to $100,000 a mile – equivalent to about $2.4 million a mile today. The plan was swiftly abandoned, and the railway departed the canyon at Cimarron to take a switchback detour over Cerro Summit.

It is encouraging to know that the Gunnison remains untamed, and that neither a railway nor a bridge has ever been built in or across the gorge. The fact that the Gunnison River still flows wild and free in its 26-mile journey through the national park somehow justifies Bryant's 19th century exasperation.

The British poet and novelist Rudyard Kipling visited the upstream part of the Black Canyon in 1889, as a passenger on the railway. His description still rings true:-

> We had been climbing for very many hours when we entered a gorge, remote from the sun, where the rocks were two thousand feet sheer and where a rock-splintered river roared and howled. There was a glory and wonder and a mystery about that mad ride which I felt keenly. We seemed to be running into the bowls of the earth at the invitation of an irresponsible stream.

The Narrows

Bryce Canyon National Park

*'Deep caverns and rooms
resembling ruins of prisons, castles,
churches with their guarded walls,
battlements, spires and steeples,
niches and recesses ...'*

T C Bailey, 1877

Evening light on Queen's Garden

Starry, starry night

A myriad twinkling stars spread over the velvety night sky like diamonds strewn across a jeweller's baize. The misty cloud of the Milky Way arced from horizon to horizon, enlivened by the occasional sudden silver streak of a shooting star and flash of lightning in the background.

Silhouetted jet-black against this celestial backdrop were the weird shapes of the hoodoos which are such an iconic feature of Bryce Canyon National Park. It was a night that will live long in my memory. We weren't even supposed to have been there. The itinerary of our 'Super-Fam' international press trip had scheduled a Country and

Kissing hoodoos

Western night at the local inn that evening. But Japanese photographer Osamu declared he wasn't going. 'I'm going back down the canyon,' he said. 'Bryce has some of the most unpolluted skies in the US, and as there's no moon tonight, I'm going to get some pictures.'

Our hosts were not best pleased, but a few of us agreed with Osamu, so we set off with just a couple of headlamps to illuminate the darkness, down the Navajo Loop Trail which we'd walked in bright sunlight earlier that day. As Osamu set up his tripod, we gazed awestruck at the unfolding panorama of the unsullied night sky. We felt truly humbled and firmly put in our place as such an insignificant part of the universe. I hadn't seen a sky like it since I was a boy in the 1950s in eastern England.

*   *   *

It may be apocryphal, but I love the story of how Mormon cattle rancher Ebenezer Bryce, while looking for stray cattle across the Paunsaugunt plateau, first came across the incredible city of obelisks, towers, arches and red sandstone cliffs of the canyon which eventually took his name. 'Gee,' exclaimed Ebenezer, raising his Stetson and scratching his head. 'That's one helluva place to lose a cow!'.

Of course, Ebenezer was not the first to come across this silent city of stone. The Paiute tribe of Native Americans thought the hoodoos were the 'Legend People' whom their deity Coyote had turned to stone.

Inspiration Point, Navajo Loop

Earlier we'd walked down into the canyon in the glowing late afternoon sun past the improbable, tottering hoodoos of Thor's Hammer and the needle-like Sentinel and through the claustrophobic canyon of Wall Street, with its twin brave Douglas firs reaching up for the light.

We walked on through to the wonderland known as the Queen's Garden, weaving between pink and orange hoodoos framed by ancient ponderosa pines and Douglas firs. As we paid homage to the plump, bustled and crowned shape of the Queen Victoria hoodoo, another of our party wandered off into one of the many side canyons. Suddenly from that direction we heard the rumble and crash of falling rocks, and saw a cloud of choking red dust rolling down towards us.

Thankfully, our friend emerged dusty but unscathed, but in that instant, we realized that Bryce Canyon was still a work in progress, and the timeless erosion which created this astonishing array of towering pinnacles continues.

Bryce Canyon – actually, it's much more of a series of amphitheaters – is the youngest in the so-called 'Grand Staircase' of gigantic, geological steps on the Colorado Plateau, uplifted around 15 million years ago. These sandstone steps start with the oldest rocks of the Grand Canyon, followed by Zion and ending at Bryce, whose Claron sandstones are a mere 33 to 53 million years old.

It was the incredulous descriptions of Bryce by early explorers such as T C Bailey in 1877 that eventually resulted in its designation as a national park in 1928. Bailey enthused:-

> *There are deep caverns and rooms resembling ruins of prisons, castles, churches with their guarded walls, battlements, spires and steeples, niches and recesses, presenting the wildest and most wonderful scene that the eye of man ever beheld, in fact it is one of the wonders of the world.*

Queen's Garden

Canyonlands National Park

'Wherever we look there is but a wilderness of rocks; deep gorges,
where the rivers are lost below cliffs and towers and pinnacles ...'

John Wesley Powell

White Rim reflections

Island in the sky

At places like the Island in the Sky mesa in Canyonlands National Park, you find yourself looking down into, rather than up at, the scenery.

As you travel across the great 7000-foot-high Colorado Plateau on the long desert roads of southern Utah and northern Arizona, you don't always see the wildest of red rock canyon country. Much of it lies hidden away where great rivers like the Colorado, the Green and their tributaries have carved out an intricate jig-saw of canyons up to 2000 feet deep into the sandstone plateau.

On his first visit, wilderness aficionado Edward Abbey claimed it was '…the splendour of the landscape, the perfection of the silence' that most impressed him. Canyonlands was, Abbey said 'the most weird, wonderful, magical place on earth – there is nothing else like it anywhere'.

Island in the Sky is the descriptive name given to the broad, flat mesa which is sandwiched between the deep canyons cut out by the Colorado to the east and the Green river to the west. It gives an astonishing red-tailed hawk's-eye view of Monument Basin and the deeply-incised course of the Green River, framed by the twisted remains of a fence of dead junipers in the foreground. The distinctive sandstone bench of the White Rim is 1200 feet below to the east, while in the background are the snow-capped La Sal, Abajos and Henry Mountains, up to 100 miles distant.

Also visible in the middle distance from the Island in the Sky viewpoint is the jagged-edged crater of the 4560-foot-high Upheaval Dome, perhaps the oddest geological feature in the park. Geologists still argue about how it was formed, with theories ranging from a volcanic origin to underground salt deposits pushing up the sandstone and a less-likely meteor hit.

Snagwood shadows, Island in the Sky

The Needles

The wildest area in wild Canyonlands National Park is without doubt The Maze, described by the Park Service as one of the most remote and inaccessible places in the US. It consists of a confusing jumble of canyons which has been described as 'a 30-square-mile puzzle in sandstone'.

Given descriptive names such as the Land of the Standing Rocks, the Doll House and The Fins, it is a bewildering wilderness of weirdly-shaped multi-colored walls, towers, buttes and mesas, where it is the easiest thing in the world to get well and truly lost.

The Needles area in the south of the park rivals The Maze in its remoteness and certainly in its physical landmarks. It is an amazing landscape of rocky canyons, spires, pinnacles, arches and natural bridges, all sculpted from the yellow and red striped Cedar Mesa sandstone.

33

The natural arches include the gargantuan Elephant Arch (which reminds me more of a Stonehenge trilithon) a short walk from the Squaw Flat campground. On the way to the campsite is Wooden Shoe Arch, a cliff-top, clog-like feature – a freestanding arch in the making.

Of Canyonlands' natural arches, the easiest to get to is the low, sweeping Mesa Arch, just a few steps off the northern entrance road to the Island in the Sky. A favorite subject for photographers, the Navajo sandstone arch neatly frames Washer Woman Arch, Airport Tower and other outlying features of the White Rim escarpment.

South of Horseshoe Canyon, a detached unit of the park, is Bluejohn Canyon. It was here in 2003 that Aron Ralston, a 27-year-old Aspen adventurer, had an accident which attracted world-wide attention. Negotiating the narrow Bluejohn slot canyon, Ralston's right arm became trapped by a falling boulder, and after an agonizing six days he took the brave decision to save himself by amputating it with his multi-tool knife.

Ralston told his harrowing story in the book *Between a Rock and Hard Place*, which was later made into the six-times Oscar-nominated film *127 Hours* by British director Danny Boyle.

So perhaps we should leave the last words to Ralston, whose love of the desert country had so nearly cost him his life, as he stood in the Doll's House:

The vista held for me a feeling of the dawn of time, that primordial epoch before life when there was only desolate land.

Twisted juniper, Grand View Point

Crater Lake National Park

The Watchman kept his stony gaze over the reflections in the lake, where ripples danced in the afternoon breeze.

Wizard Island, The Watchman and Llao Rock

Mazama blues

'Blue' is a totally inadequate word to describe the color of Crater Lake. And a search through the thesaurus doesn't help. You can't really call it azure or cerulean, like the sky; aquamarine, like a sun-lit sea; or sapphire, like lapis lazuli – although it must be said, in certain light, it is any of these.

Even Freeman Tilden, perhaps the greatest interpreter of the US National Parks, had to admit that the blue of Crater Lake was not the blue of anything – except, that is, the unique blue of Crater Lake itself.

The first sight of the 21-square-mile caldera lake ringed by towering 2000-foot cliffs rising above its limpid surface is one that I'll never forget. We had made the 80-mile drive from Roseburg through the Umpqua National Forest and across the barren 6000-foot-high Pumice Desert.

When we arrived at the Merriam Point pull-out on the north west rim, we just stood speechless for several minutes, marvelling at this sublime example of the power and beauty of Nature. We couldn't argue with its frequent description as the most beautiful lake in the world.

The placid lake, so unexpected at this altitude, spread out before us with the mural precipices of Llao Rock to the left and across to Cloudcap Bay over the water on the far side, with Dutton Cliff and 8929-foot Mt Scott beyond. Closer at hand, the perfect forested cone of Wizard Island was guarded by the 8013-foot peak of The Watchman.

The caldera of Crater Lake – at 1900 feet the deepest freshwater lake in the US – was formed by the cataclysmic eruption of the former mile-high Mt Mazama about 7000 years ago. The last of a series of eruptions – which blasted some

The volcanic plug of Phantom Ship

Wizard Island in winter

25 cubic miles of ash and magma into the sky – was 42 times greater than the eruption of Mt St Helens in 1980, blanketing ash over 500,000 square miles, as far away as Idaho, California, Nevada and Wyoming.

The lake may be idyllically peaceful now, but the more recent, 6000-year-old cinder cone of Wizard Island, and the eroded spires of the Phantom Ship in the south east corner of the lake, served to remind us of that we were in the presence of a sleeping giant.

After a drive along the western rim skirting the slopes of Hillman Peak and The Watchman, we reached Rim Village and the Sinnott Memorial overlook, honoring Nicholas J Sinnott, the

Oregon senator who was instrumental in creating the Crater Lake National Park. I was also pleased to see a memorial plaque to Stephen T Mather, the wealthy Chicago industrialist and national park lover, who became the inspirational first director of the National Park Service a century ago.

We returned to take the mile-long zigzag trail that descends 720 feet through the forest to Cleetwood Cove and the dock on the lake shore for the ferry which crosses Skell Channel to Wizard Island. This smaller cone is actually a volcano within a volcano, formed inside the enormous caldera about 1000 to 6000 years ago.

The dusty, cinder-choked, 1½-mile hike from Fumarole Bay through the gnarled whitebark pines and hemlocks to the 764-foot summit of the volcanic cone was tough and unrelenting. Eventually we made the 300-foot-wide summit crater and enjoyed a picnic lunch by a skeletal hemlock.

The views were truly awe-inspiring. Close at hand across the cinder reefs of Skell Channel, the volcanic ribs and the sweeping dykes and screes known as The Devil's Backbone were cast into deep relief by the lowering sun. The Watchman kept his stony gaze over the reflections in the lake, where ripples danced in the afternoon breeze.

* * *

The original discoverers of Crater Lake had unimaginatively called it Deep Blue or just plain Blue Lake. We agreed this name did no justice at all to the unique, indescribable blue of Crater Lake – the mountain that used to be.

Penstemon blooms on the crater rim

Grand Canyon National Park

'The earth suddenly sinks at our feet to illimitable depths.'

Clarence E Dutton, 1882

Evening light on Wotan's Throne, North Rim

A sublime experience

Our friends could see the disappointment written all over my face as we drove up to Point Imperial on the North Rim of the Grand Canyon. Billowing clouds of gray smoke from the raging forest fires on the Walhalla Plateau drifted across the view, obscuring the blade-like peak of Mt Hayden.

Seeing that the wind was blowing south, I guessed the areas to the west should be smoke-free. I'd read quite a bit about the Grand Canyon beforehand; I was keen to see the views from Point Sublime, familiar only from William Holmes's superb topographic engravings in Clarence Dutton's magisterial *Tertiary History of the Grand Cañon District* (1882).

I also knew that from Point Sublime you could see the canyon almost as its Spanish discoverer, Don Vazquez de Coronado, had seen it four centuries ago, without crowds, hotels or handrails like those at Point Imperial or on the more populous South Rim. The only practical way to reach Point Sublime was a tortuous, 18-mile forestry track which wound in and out of the edge of the Kaibab Plateau from North Rim village.

We kicked up a lot of dust as we rocked and rolled our way through and over fallen trees, in and out of creeks and spinning in deep ruts as we headed west across the plateau. When we eventually reached the isolated headland of Point Sublime, we realized that Dutton's name and description were no exaggeration. Exactly as he described it: 'The earth suddenly sinks at our feet to illimitable depths. In an instant, in the twinkling of an eye, the awful scene is before us'.

Dawn light on Mt Hayden

Canyon architecture through a natural window

The foreground, as in Holmes's engraving, was punctuated by the tall, nodding seed heads of yuccas and the occasional gnarled and salmon-trunked pinyon pine. Beyond, a feast of architectural rock formations met the eye. Alcoves and amphitheaters constructed from the strata of 300-million-year-old sandstones were buttressed by fans of spreading scree and painted in a kaleidoscope of glowing colors, ranging from the richest magenta to yellow, pink and vermillion.

Point Sublime is also one of the few places on either rim where you can actually see the Colorado River, the architect of that grand window into the unfathomable depths of geological time. The glistening silver stream looked tiny and insignificant from our lofty viewpoint a mile above the chasm.

Most people see the Grand Canyon in the heat of a summer day, when it is often filled by a dense heat haze. Luckily, it was mid-

41

afternoon by the time we left Point Sublime, the shadows were lengthening and we were privileged to witness what Dutton described as the canyon 'coming to life':

> *The slumber of the chasm is disturbed. The temples and cloisters seem to raise themselves half awake to greet the passing shadow. Their wilted, dropping, flattened faces expand into relief. The long promontories reach out from the distant wall as if to catch a moment's refreshment from the shade. The colors begin to glow; the haze loses its opaque density and becomes more tenuous.*

Not a bad evocation for a serious scientific monograph. Dutton's descriptions rival Thomas Moran's epic landscape paintings, which did so much to persuade Congress to create the world's first national park at Yellowstone in 1872.

It was one-armed Civil War veteran Major John Wesley Powell who appointed Dutton as geologist to the US Geological Survey, and it was Powell who first explored the length of the Grand Canyon in 1869. With an unlikely ragtag team of nine mountain men, he entered 'the great unknown' and became the first to shoot the formidable rapids of the Colorado and travel the full 277 miles of the gorge between the Green and Virgin Rivers.

When the Grand Canyon was first proposed for federal protection in 1903, President Theodore Roosevelt visited the great natural wonder and wisely urged:

> *Leave it as it is. The ages have been at work on it, and Man can only mar it. What you can do is to keep it for your children, your children's children and for all who come after you, as one of the great sights which every American, if he can travel at all, should see.*

Rimrock, Point Sublime

Grand Teton National Park

*Glorious flower-filled upland meadows
and cool forests of sweet-smelling conifers …*

A meadowland bouquet of goldeneye and geranium

Mountain wonderland

The shuttle ferry across the mirror-calm waters of Jenny Lake to the West Shore Boat Dock was a beautiful introduction, with the triple snow-clad peaks of the Grand Tetons beckoning to the west. My destination, the deep cleft of Cascade Canyon between The Jaw and Teewinot Mountain, struck up directly into their very heart.

Disembarking, I followed the path as it climbed steadily through the trees until a thunderous roar gave away the location of Hidden Falls, 50 yards away to the left. It was probably this pretty, 200-foot cascade over the hard, metamorphic rocks which gave the creek and canyon its name, and it is obviously a popular stopping off place on the trail. As I watched, a white-bibbed dipper flashed across the tumbling waterfall in its constant underwater quest for insect larvae.

The trail crossed the creek by a wooden footbridge and then traversed a rock face to reach Inspiration Point, the apparent destination for most tourists. Sheltering under an overhanging rock and shaded by pines, it provides a grandstand view over Jenny Lake, its pine-covered glacial moraine formed by the ancient Cascade Canyon glacier, and the peaks of Shadow Mountain, Sleeping Indian Mountain, Signal Mountain and the Mt Leidy highlands far away to the east.

Returning to the trail, I started the gentle climb through thimbleberry bushes, the spikey blue flowers of silky phacelia and multi-colored columbines, to reach the entrance portals of Cascade Canyon.

Cascade Canyon, Mt Owen in the background

Dawn reflections in Beaver Pond, Schwabacher's Landing

Having been warned on the ferry about the presence of bears, I made sure to make plenty of noise as I strode through the undergrowth.

Over the next few miles, the ruler-straight, east-west canyon gradually opened out, revealing increasingly impressive views south to the rocky, snow-topped spires of the so-called 'Cathedral Group' of Teewinot Mountain (12,325 ft) and Mt Owen (12,928 ft); eventually I caught glimpses of the reigning peak of Grand Teton (13,770 ft) towering beyond.

As I passed beneath Storm Point (10,054 ft) and the Rock of Ages to my right, the trail crossed open fields of enormous,

45

glacier-transported boulders (talus); the whistle of inquisitive yellow-bellied marmots and the bleat of pikas heralded my passing, and they scampered away as I approached. This was followed by glorious flower-filled upland meadows and cool forests of sweet-smelling conifers and Douglas fir, with a rich understorey of serviceberry, raspberry, huckleberry, honeysuckle and mountain ash. Ahead beckoned the comb-carved crest of The Wigwams.

The climb through this mountain wonderland was gradual and easy, and I soon passed the impressive gash of Valhalla Canyon to the left, which gave a dramatic foreground to the dominant spire of Grand Teton. Avalanche chutes and apparently-recent rock falls indicated that I had really entered mountain country now.

Crossing a footbridge over Cascade Creek at around 8000 feet, I soon reached the fork that in one direction led to the remote cirque which holds Solitude Lake (9035 ft), or, in the other, along the Teton Crest Trail to Hurricane Pass. But I had a ferry to catch, so reluctantly had to turn back to retrace my steps and descend Cascade Canyon.

My introduction to the range was Ansel Adams' moody, *contre jour* shot of the winding Snake River leading the eye towards the snowy Tetons (1942). Adams once said, and it's a view that David Muench shares: 'A great photograph is one that fully expresses what one feels, in the deepest sense, about what is being photographed.'

And as Freeman Tilden wrote in *The National Parks* (1951):

> *To see the Tetons mirrored in Jackson Lake early on a clear summer morning when not a breath of wind is stirring and the image of the range is so sharply defined that its identical twin lives in the water – this is an experience never to be forgotten in discovering the real America.*

Cathedral Group: Middle Teton, Grand Teton and Mt Teewinot

Deep in that canyon and near its head are many houses of the old people – the Ancient Ones.

Spruce Tree House

Rooms with a view

Our Hopi ranger guide in the Mesa Verde National Park kept a dead straight face as he asked if we had heard about the 32-foot ladder we needed to climb to reach the ruins of Balcony House.

Yes, we nodded, we all knew about the ladder. 'Good,' replied the ranger, 'Now, how many have experience of rappelling?' A few of us gingerly put up our hands and walked to one side as he indicated.

'You see, what isn't usually explained is that we have to rappel to get back out again' continued the ranger. At this point, none but the bravest shuffled across to join the larger, more inexperienced group. Then the penny dropped, and laughter was tinged with relief as we realized he was pulling our legs.

In all honesty, the wide, wooden-slatted ladder to reach Balcony House was no more dangerous than a domestic step ladder. The tight little 12-foot-long tunnel we needed to crawl through to exit was much more challenging.

Mesa Verde – Spanish for 'green table' – was designated in 1906 and is unique among American national parks in that it preserves human culture and buildings as opposed to scenery and wildlife.

Having said that, it occupies a spectacular natural situation on a broad, rolling mesa 2000 feet above Colorado's Montezuma and Mancos Valleys. This is best appreciated from Park Point, the summit viewpoint at 8571 ft, on the North Rim of the mesa which offers a 360° panorama. When considering making Mesa Verde a national park in 1905, Congress referred to this as 'one of the grandest and most extensive views in the country'.

Cliff Palace

Yucca and Long House, Wetherill Mesa

On a clear day, the view takes in the distant La Sal Mountains in Utah, 110 miles to the north; the La Plata Mountains of Colorado to the east; Shiprock in New Mexico and the Lukachukai Mountains in Arizona to the south; and the distinctive profile of Sleeping Ute Mountain across the Montezuma Valley to the west.

However, the Ancestral Puebloans who about 800 years ago built the 600 famous cliff dwellings of Mesa Verde were interested in more than the view. From about AD 500-750, they grouped their dwellings into pueblos, or villages, on the mesa top, at places such as Far View, Pipe Shrine House and the Sun Temple.

From about AD 1200, they started to move down into the large, overhung alcoves in the canyon walls, possibly for defensive reasons when they were threatened by hostile rival tribes. They constructed their many-roomed houses, towers up to four storeys

49

high, and circular, underground kivas (places used for religious rituals) in the easily-defensible hidden terraces which Nature had carved out of the pink-brown Cretaceous sandstone.

The most famous is Cliff Palace, the largest cliff dwelling in North America. It contains 217 rooms and 23 kivas, and probably housed about 250 people during the 13th century. It was named by Mancos Valley cowboys Richard Wetherill and his brother-in-law Charlie Mason, who were the first white men to see it.

Acowitz, a member of the Ute tribe, had told Wetherill of a special cliff dwelling in Mesa Verde: 'Deep in that canyon and near its head are many houses of the old people – the Ancient Ones. One of those houses, high, high in the rocks, is bigger than all the others. Utes never go there, it is a sacred place.'

One snowy, December day in 1888 when Wetherill and Mason were riding across the mesa looking for stray cattle, they came across the 'magnificent city' which they dubbed 'Cliff Palace'. Later, they excavated artefacts and camped in the ruins for days and weeks at a time, leading sightseeing tours for visitors.

It's easy to imagine families of Ancestral Puebloans living in their high-rise villages when you look down from Cliff Palace onto Soda Canyon – a scene virtually unchanged from what they must have known. The view from Balcony House, 600 feet above the canyon, is even more spectacular, and the 40 or 50 people who lived in its 40 rooms must have felt safe and secure.

But, for reasons still not fully understood, the spectacular cliff dwellings of Mesa Verde were occupied for only about 75 to 100 years, and by AD 1300 had been abandoned – to await their rediscovery by those astonished cowboys nearly six centuries later.

Balcony House kiva

Monument Valley Navajo Tribal Park

Mitten Rocks and Merrick Butte

'Monument Valley is the place where earth and sky join in harmony and beauty.'

David Muench, 2015

Standing up country

Monument Valley, the butte and mesa studded Navajo Nation Tribal Park which straddles the Arizona-Utah border, is probably everyone's romantic ideal of the great American West.

Used as a backdrop to countless movies from John Ford's classic *Stagecoach* in 1938 to *Forrest Gump* and *Back to the Future Part III*, and in hundreds of TV and magazine ads, it prompted the distinguished film critic Keith Phipps to observe: '…its five square miles have defined what decades of moviegoers think of when they imagine the American West'.

Monument Valley also holds a very special place in David Muench's heart. His father Josef had prepared an album of black-and-white photographs of the valley for his good friend

Summer clouds in Monument Valley

and valley ambassador Harry Goulding of Goulding's Trading Post. This was instrumental in attracting Ford to Monument Valley, and many, many others since.

As David writes of the Gouldings in the Preface to his 2015 book *Monument Valley*: 'In welcoming my parents and me into their world, they provided the small child I was with what I now understand as among the most powerful of my formative experiences. … For me, Monument Valley is the place where earth and sky join in harmony and beauty.'

For many visitors the Gouldings personified the way-out-West character of the valley. Harry came to Monument Valley in a Model-T Ford in 1923, initially setting up as a sheep-herder and later building his trading post – now a recognized national landmark and visitor center – on the western edge of the valley beneath the Big Rock Door Mesa.

Harry chose the site wisely. It was sheltered from the wind and sun by the rock wall behind, and the view from the front porch was one to die for. Extending for up to 65 miles, it includes

Yei Bi Chei, with Totem Pole at centre right

the buttes and mesas of Train Rock, Eagle Rock, Brigham's Tomb (named for the Mormon leader Ellis Brigham), Big Leader, Big Indian and Castle Buttes.

Superlatives abound in descriptions of this amazing landscape. Navajos, rather matter-of-factly, call it *Tsé Bii' Ndzisgaii*, meaning 'the valley of the rocks', but a century ago, writing in *Pacific Monthly*, WC McBride accurately observed of the Utah and Arizona red rock desert: 'There is as much country standing up as there is laying down'.

Access to the valley today is strictly in the company of Navajo guides. I went in an open-topped jeep across the Mitchell Butte Wash and past the iconic Sentinel Mesa, North and South Mittens and Merrick Butte to reach the traditional 'photo opportunity' – inevitably known as John Ford Point.

Tribe members had set up their stalls selling traditional silver and turquoise jewellery, rugs and blankets, and a horse rider conveniently adopted a typical John Wayne pose on the eroded headland. Sentinel Mesa, West Mitten Butte, Big Indian, Merrick Butte and the Castle Rock-Stagecoach group formed a suitably dramatic backdrop.

We travelled on past the pinnacles of the Three Sisters (which our guide said formed a 'W' for welcome to visitors) and through the narrow arroyo between the Rain God and Thunderbird Mesas. In the distance, we could just make out the Totem Pole among the group of spires and mesa known as *Yei Bi Chei ('the holy people')*. Further in the distance were the cliffs of *Tse biyi yazzi* ('little valley within the rocks') and Hunt's Mesa.

The Totem Pole is a needle-like 450-feet-high red sandstone column only 40 feet wide, recognisable from the opening sequences of Clint Eastwood's 1975 movie, *The Eiger Sanction*, in which Eastwood and George Kennedy were filmed on its vertiginous top. Apparently it has been off-limits to climbers ever since.

Contorted junipers, purple sage, yellow rabbit brush and snakewood somehow wrested an existence from the burning desert sands under the towering buttes and mesas. I was fascinated to see a large black scarab beetle scuttling across the desert floor.

Harry Goulding once said when he saw a cloud of dust from a speeding car traversing the valley floor: 'That's probably some darn fool who *thinks* he's seeing Monument Valley.' As I discovered, you really have to get some sand in your boots to appreciate the glories of magnificent Monument Valley.

Totem Pole, waxing moon

55

Mt Hood Wilderness

Mt Hood reflected in Lost Lake

It is everyone's idea of what a volcano should look like, a perfect, snow-clad cone rising in splendid, stately isolation from the surrounding forest.

Metlako Falls, Eagle Creek

57

Cathartic Cascades

The flags were flying at half-mast over Timberline Lodge, 6000 feet up on the slopes of Mt Hood in the Oregon Cascades, and the snowy slopes of the craggy, 11,249 ft summit stood out boldly against the crystal-clear blue of the sky. It was some time before we realized what was different. There was not a single aircraft contrail in sight.

It was the morning of Tuesday, September 11, 2001 – a date indelibly stamped on recent US history after the horrific terrorist attacks on New York and Washington – and the whole of the nation's civilian airspaces was closed.

We had just arrived in Portland, Oregon, and were about to embark on a carefully-planned marathon tour of US national parks. But after watching with mounting disbelief the traumatic events of that morning live on TV, the trip looked very much in doubt. The nation was in a state of shock, as an unprecedented sense of self-doubt swept through the country, soon to be replaced by a mood of defiance.

Fortunately, that was the mood of our hosts, Homer and Deanna, as we set out on the first leg of our journey to the Cascade peaks of Mt Hood and Mt St Helens. As we travelled east through the old growth forests of the Cascades, the leaves of the hardwoods were just starting to turn, the scarlet of the maples contrasting with the gold of the aspens, and the rivers still burst their boisterous way down from the mountains. The natural world cared not one jot for the madness of mankind and continued on as it always had, in its quiet, healing way.

In many ways, we were delighted to see that the unforgettable morning had a cathartic effect on our American friends – reaffirming their love of their wonderful wildernesses that they wanted to share with us.

Maples and ferns, Columbia River gorge

Rhododendrons frame Mt Hood

Mt Hood, known by the Multnomah tribe as Wy'est after a mountain deity, is the highest point in Oregon and a prominent landmark from Portland, 50 miles to the west. It is everyone's idea of what a volcano should look like, a perfect, snow-clad cone rising in splendid, stately isolation from the surrounding forest.

But it is also a potentially-active stratovolcano which last erupted in 1865, and it is still considered by the US Geological Survey as 'dormant but potentially active' – of all Oregon volcanoes, the most likely to erupt. Thankfully, I didn't feel any rumblings as I ascended the lower slopes from Timberline Lodge towards the beckoning snowline and the Silcox Hut, through fields of purple lupines and wind-blasted skeletal trees.

Mt Hood is home to a dozen named glaciers and snowfields and there are 3600 feet of ski runs, no less than six ski chairlifts and over seven square miles of skiable territory on its southern slopes, including the 'groomed' slopes of the snowfield below the Palmer Glacier.

Timberline Lodge itself is a rustic masterpiece of Arts and Crafts architecture. It was built from 1936-8, at the heart of the Great Depression, by over 100 out-of-work craftsmen of the Works Progress Administration (WPA) set up by President Franklin D Roosevelt.

The shingled-roofed building stands on the south-eastern shoulder of the mountain like a cathedral to the Great Outdoors. Its central conical tower is topped by a brass and bronze weathervane that is a modern interpretation of an Ancestral Puebloan pictogram of a wild bird. It now serves as the logo for the lodge.

Inside, a mammoth hexagonal dressed-stone fireplace dominates the lobby, where six massive wooden columns support the encircling mezzanine. The columns were logged from Washington's Gifford Pinchot National Forest, and hand-carved using broad axes and foot adzes.

Mt Hood Wilderness, including Timberline Lodge, is one of eight wilderness areas within the Mt Hood National Forest which extends south from the Columbia River gorge over more than 100 square miles of forested mountains, lakes and streams.

We enjoyed afternoon tea in the Lodge before travelling back to Portland via the impressive, 542-foot single drop Multnomah Falls in the broad Columbia Valley. This was where the pioneering Corps of Discovery, led by Meriwether Lewis and William Clark, finally reached their goal of the Pacific Ocean, after their epic transcontinental adventure in November 1805.

Clouds clearing from Mt Hood

Mt Rainier National Park

The lakes lived up to their name by perfectly reflecting the massive, glacier-clad south face of the mountain in the still, ice-blue waters.

Mt Rainier reflected in Tipsoo Lake

The mountain

Ron Warfield – author, photographer and former assistant chief park naturalist – was emphatic about Rainier. 'It's *the* mountain,' he exclaimed. 'Where else do they speak of *the* mountain?'

Ron was on duty behind the counter at the mile-high Henry M Jackson Memorial Visitor Center at the aptly-named Paradise Meadows. He left us in no doubt about his regard for his favorite mountain, proudly showing me his amazing photograph of a dramatic lenticular cloud hanging like a glowing anvil over the summit.

The 14,410-foot snow-capped summit of Rainier stands in splendid isolation at the northern end of the Cascades. It supports the largest glacier system in the contiguous US, and is one of the world's most massive volcanoes. The mountain and its national park cover a total area of 368 square miles, and you can see its snowy slopes from over 100 miles away as you approach through dense, old forests from Portland.

Rainier is the highest of the volcanic Cascades, a link in the so-called 'Ring of Fire' which encircles the mighty Pacific Ocean. Although Rainier has not had a major eruption for more than a century, the constantly steaming fumaroles and vents near the summit craters of Liberty Cap and Point Success indicate that it is only sleeping, and the US Geological Survey has to keep a constant watch on the simmering summit.

Lupines and daisies, Yakima Park

Fall foliage, Mt Rainier

Whilst it lacks the shapely cone of nearby Mt Hood, Rainier more than makes up for that in its beautiful setting. Most people enter the park from the Nisqually entrance through the old-growth forests of Douglas fir, cedar, alder and hemlock to Longmire and up the Paradise Valley via Cougar Rock and the 168-foot cascade of the Narada Falls to Paradise Meadows.

Longmire takes its name from being the site of James Longmire's Medical Springs, set up in 1888. As we approached, the smart clerical gray of Clark's nutcrackers and the electric blue of Steller's jays enlivened the forest scene at every pull-out.

The subalpine meadows of Paradise Valley were apparently so-named by Longmire's daughter-in-law Martha, who on her first visit exclaimed: 'Wow. This must be what Paradise is like.' The meadows come into glorious life in mid-June, and by July, a profusion of up to 40 species of wildflowers have been recorded.

They range from the sky-blue of Lyall's lupines to the luminous scarlet of paintbrush, vivid pink fireweed and white valerians and bistorts, all of which thrive in the rich, undisturbed volcanic soil. Towards fall, the tiny leaves of the Cascade huckleberry first turn yellow then bright red. The taste of their luscious blue-black berries is appropriately reflected in the plant's Latin name, *Vaccinium deliciosum*.

Our brief stroll through the meadows from Paradise Lodge took us around the Mazama Ridge and down to Reflection Lakes, which nestle in a basin carved out by one of Rainier's many historic glaciers. It was a fine day, and the lakes lived up to their name by perfectly reflecting the massive, glacier-clad south face of the mountain in the still, ice-blue waters, with the Cowlitz Glacier, Gibraltar Rock and Point Success standing out prominently.

We understood, as we walked back to Paradise, why Ron Warfield had referred to Rainier as '*the* mountain'.

Mt Rainier from Indian Henry's Hunting Ground

Mt St Helens National Volcanic Monument

... the former perfect, symmetrical volcanic cone of Mt St Helens.

Spirit Lake and Mt St Helens before the eruption

Above Spirit Lake, beargrass blooms after the eruption

Ashes to ashes

Twenty years on, the scene was still one of utter devastation. Acre upon acre of bone-white, skeletal trees lay scattered in neat rows across the gray hillsides, like huge matchsticks blown over by a giant's breath. Those trees still left standing were shattered and splintered as if they'd been hit by a hurricane.

The hillsides themselves were still covered in a thick, choking blanket of ash. It was more like a scene from the surface of the Moon than the once-verdant slopes of what had been dubbed 'the Fujiyama of America' – the former perfect, symmetrical volcanic cone of Mt St Helens.

The eruption of 18 May 1980 changed all that. Five hundred times more powerful than the atomic bomb dropped on Hiroshima in World War 2, it effectively demolished the north flank of the mountain and deposited a dense cloud of volcanic ash as far as Montana, Minnesota and Oklahoma.

The huge crater in the north face

The bubbling cauliflower ash cloud was pushed 15 miles into the sky where the jet stream carried it across the nation, and eventually around the world. On a visit to the mountain soon after the eruption, President Jimmy Carter famously said: 'It makes the surface of the Moon look like a golf course'.

The 1980 eruption was the greatest and most destructive volcanic eruption in the modern history of the US. It killed 57 people, 1500 elk, 5000 deer and millions of fish, destroyed 230 square miles of forest and damaged property worth an estimated $1.5 billion. But as we travelled up the

52-mile Spirit Lake Memorial Highway, constructed between 1992-95, we saw that Nature was well advanced in her recovery. First stop was the Elk Rock viewpoint, where the full extent of the 1980 eruption could readily be appreciated. Directly below us, the valley of the North Fork of the Toutle River was still buried under 600 feet of avalanche debris and covered over by more than 100 feet of pyroclastic flow deposits – the so-called pumice plain.

Fully 10 miles from the mountain, three million cubic miles of debris and meltwater had flowed downstream at speeds of up to 60 mph and at temperatures of over 100°F for another five miles west of Elk Rock.

Using the telescope provided at the pull-out, we soon picked out a small herd of Roosevelt elk led by a magnificent stag in the valley below. Elk and deer have returned in large numbers, grazing the emergent lupines, fireweed and foxgloves, and even baby Noble firs and spruces were by now well established. By 1983, it was estimated that 90 per cent of the plant species originally growing on Mt St Helens had returned – tribute to the benign healing power of Mother Nature.

At the head of the valley, we could see the brooding presence of Mt St Helens' cratered summit, diminished from 9677 to 8365 feet. To its left was the humped shape of Harry's Ridge, with the elevated, re-shaped and debris-ridden Spirit Lake hidden behind.

The ridge takes its name from one of the most famous victims of the eruption, the colorful Harry Randall Truman, owner and caretaker at St Helen's Lodge on the shores of Spirit Lake. When the first rumblings of the mountain alerted the authorities, 83-year-old Harry stubbornly refused to leave his home of 54 years, and his 'Hell no, I'm not going' spirit captivated the nation.

Eventually, still five miles from the crater, we reached Johnston Ridge, named after a young geologist employed by the US Geological Survey to keep a watch on the simmering mountain from the top of the Coldwater Creek

Scarlet paintbrush returning above Spirit Lake

Ridge, 1200 feet above the river. Johnston's chilling last radio transmission at 8:33 am May 18, 1980 was: 'Vancouver, Vancouver, this is it!' followed by silence.

Johnston Ridge directly faces the gigantic horseshoe-shaped scar left by the 1980 eruption, and we could clearly see the 1000-foot emerging new volcanic dome which has formed inside the crater. A helpful ranger explained that what we had first thought were fumaroles rising from the summit crater were actually dust from rock falls coming from the rising dome.

'Will Mt St Helens erupt again?' we wondered. 'The answer is almost certainly yes' replied the ranger.

Sequoia & Kings Canyon National Park

The bright early morning sun illuminated the soft, fibrous trunks of the towering trees, their huge, ribbed buttresses springing from their bulbous feet.

Bulbous feet of a giant sequoia

In the company of giants

It was a crisp, early March morning and overnight snow and frost made every surface scintillate in the bright sunlight. We'd risen early from the John Muir Lodge in Grant Grove Village in Kings Canyon National Park because we wanted to beat the crowds to the Big Attraction.

The General Grant sequoia in Grant Grove is not the largest tree in the world – the General Sherman, whom we were to visit later that morning, is slightly bigger. But it is probably the best known because in 1926, President Calvin Coolidge proclaimed it the 'Nation's Christmas Tree'; and 30 years later, President Dwight D Eisenhower declared it a national living shrine to those who had died in war.

As we marched down the snow-banked trail towards the General, the contrast between the drifts of pure white snow and the warm cinnamon of the trunks of the massive sequoias was stunning. The bright early morning sun illuminated the soft, fibrous trunks of the towering trees, their huge, ribbed buttresses springing from the virginal snow at their bulbous feet. It was a magical moment which we had all to ourselves, and we felt totally insignificant in this company of giants.

We watched fascinated as white-tailed mule deer gambolled through the aisles of this cathedral of nature, seemingly unconcerned at our presence. Pikas squeaked their warning calls as we passed, and we heard the occasional raucous chatter of an electric-blue Steller's jay. No other sounds disturbed the primordial peace of the forest.

Sequoia's winter wonderland

Many of these giants bore the jet-black scars of lightning strikes and fires, termed 'catfaces' by loggers, who thankfully now leave these monsters alone. Frequent fires seem to do no harm at all to the thick-barked sequoia, clearing the ground beneath and making room for young trees to grow in the fertile soil.

The General Sherman tree in Giant Forest in the adjoining Sequoia National Park is the world's largest living tree. It is also one of the oldest sequoias, with an estimated age of 2300 to 2700 years. That means it was a seedling during the Iron Age, before the Romans came to Britain.

The astonishing thing is that this giant grew from a seed no bigger than an oat flake, encapsulated in a cone the size of a partridge egg. It was a humbling experience to stand beneath its 40-foot diameter trunk and look up at branches eight-foot thick – branches that would have made a sizeable trunk on lesser trees.

We drove through the fallen Tunnel Log sequoia on our way to Moro Rock, a 6725-foot granite monolith on the southern edge of the park. After a steep, 400-step climb, we reached the bald, dome-like summit, which commanded a breathtaking view south across blue, receding ridges towards the snow-capped peaks of the Sierra Nevada. Unfortunately, the intervening ranges blocked our view of the reigning peak of Mt Whitney, at 14,505 feet the highest mountain in the contiguous 48 states.

Yucca flowers, Moro Rock

71

Kearsarge Pinnacles, Kings Canyon

We took the Kings Canyon Scenic Byway, past Boyden Cave, Grizzly Falls and Cedar Grove village to get a glimpse into the mountain fastnesses of the Kings Canyon National Park. The Roaring River, whose headwaters rise to the south in the ominous Deadman Canyon, crashed over its eponymous falls to join the equally-boisterous, copper-green waters of the Kings River near Knapp's Cabin.

This charming little shingle-roofed one-roomed shack was built on a raised glacial moraine in 1925 by George Owen Knapp, founder of the industrial giant, Union Carbide. Knapp used the cabin for storage while camping in the area. In the 1950s, the National Park Service assumed its maintenance and it was added to the National Register of Historic Places in 1978.

Unfortunately, we only had time to reach the Alpine setting of flower-studded Zumwalt Meadow, spectacular beneath the granite guardians of 8717-foot North Dome and the 8518-foot Grand Sentinel, and the Road's End. Our planned hike to Mist Falls on the Paradise Valley Trail would have to wait for another day.

It was the first Spanish explorers led by Gabriel Moraga, searching for a mission site, who named the mighty Kings River and its associated canyon *El Rio de los Santos Reyes* – 'the River of the Holy Kings'.

As we left this park of superlatives, we couldn't argue with that divinely regal description.

Foxtail pine and University Peak, Kings Canyon

Shenandoah National Park

Jefferson was fond of this place and spent time here quietly contemplating the wonders of Nature.

Top of Dark Hollow Falls

Seeing the wood for the trees

It seemed ironic that the ranger-led walk from Big Meadows in Shenandoah National Park showed us the remains of where the original inhabitants of these ancient Blue Ridge Mountains once lived. When the park was designated in 1935, about 400 'hillbilly' families, described as being 'almost completely cut off from the current of American life' were evicted to make room for the park, in the mistaken belief that all national parks had to be uninhabited wildernesses like Yosemite and Yellowstone in the West.

That was many years ago, and thankfully the park's original authoritarian attitude is long gone. The important cultural history of the area is now recognized and explained in visitor centers. The action of the Government in evicting these hard-working families really hit the headlines. They had lived there in harmony with the landscape for several generations, and many refused to leave quietly.

Apart from the significance of its cultural heritage, Shenandoah National Park is important in many other ways. An estimated 50 million people live within a day's drive and it receives over two million visits a year. It was the first national park to be situated close to the large population centers of the east coast and of Washington DC, which is just 75 miles away.

It was President Franklin D Roosevelt's 'New Deal' Civilian Conservation Corps (CCC) public work relief program that

Fall leaves

created the national park that we see today. Between 1933 and 1942, ten CCC camps including Big Meadow were established within Shenandoah, and at any one time more than 1000 boys and young men were working here.

Their tasks included the building of trails, fire roads and towers, comfort stations, picnic grounds and construction projects associated with the 105-mile Skyline Drive, which runs along the granite crest of the Blue Ridge Mountains. Its name changes to Blue Ridge Parkway as

Richland Balsam Overlook, Blue Ridge Parkway

it leaves the park at Rockfish Gap. Most visitors follow this road especially during the fall or 'foliage' season. The various pull-outs constructed by the CCC also afford spectacular views and easy trails take you to the bald granite tops of peaks such as Stony Man, Bearfence and Old Rag Mountains.

Over nine years, three million young men participated in the CCC, which provided them with shelter, clothing, and food, together with a modest wage of $30 a month – $25 of which had to be sent home to their families. A life-size bronze statue of a typical ax-wielding CCC workman stands in front of the Harry F Byrd Visitor Center at Big Meadows, commemorating the men and boys of the Corps.

I left the ranger walk to take the short descent to the pretty 70-foot cascade of the Dark Hollow Falls, hidden among the greenstone rocks of Dark Hollow. It is thought that President Thomas Jefferson was fond of this place and spent time here quietly contemplating the wonders of Nature. Maybe this was where he first considered that protecting the American environment should be a national goal – a thought he expressed in his *Notes on the State of Virgina (1785)*.

It was an atmospheric, misty day on my visit, and I felt at one with the third president and Founding Father as I explored the falls from top to bottom, and heard the melodious 'look-up, look-up' call of a fellow summer visitor, the blue-headed vireo.

Just over 100 miles of the 2200-mile Appalachian Trail runs parallel to the

Dark Hollow Falls

Skyline Drive through Shenandoah National Park. Wanting to get just a taste of this famous marathon walk, I took the Rose River Loop Trail to Fishers Gap and then followed the white-daubed waymarkers of the trail to return to Big Meadows.

This grand-daddy among National Scenic Trails was conceived by Benton MacKaye, a former forester and planner, who came up with the idea in 1921 as an escape from the evils of modern life and 'a moral equivalent to war.' The first section opened in 1923, but it

was to take decades of patient negotiation by the Appalachian Trail Conservancy (founded in 1925) to complete the entire route.

As I drove back to our lodgings along the Skyline Drive that evening, I came across a group of visitors who had parked their cars and were eagerly pointing their cameras into the forest. I jumped out, thinking that a bear or deer had been spotted. But when I asked what they were looking at, the simple answer came back: 'Trees'.

Summit of Bearfence Mountain

Waterton-Glacier National Park

... the most transparent, crystal-clear water, revealing a mosaic of smooth, water-worn pebbles

St Mary's Lake

Grinnell Point reflected in Swiftcurrent Lake

Across the Great Divide

We'd just arrived at the 100-year-old Many Glacier Hotel, splendidly situated on the shores of Swiftcurrent Lake in the mountain heart of Glacier National Park. From our fourth floor balcony, we were admiring the stupendous views of the snow-striped face of Mt Gould (9553 ft) and the conical peak of Grinnell Point across the lake.

Then we noticed that many of our fellow guests down on the terrace in front of the hotel were staring out across the lake towards what seemed to be the opposite shore. I guessed it was a bear, because we'd already had a distant glimpse of one, plus a party of some pure-white mountain goats, way up on the slopes of Apikuni Mountain as we'd approached the hotel.

Straining my eyes, I still couldn't see anything, but the people below us seemed to be getting excited. Then I realized that they weren't looking at the far shore, but at the lake itself. And there, swimming directly towards the hotel, was the bobbing head of a brown bear.

Grabbing my camera, I rushed downstairs to get a closer look, and found that a crowd had gathered. The bear, which looked quite young and disorientated, came ashore right outside the hotel. Two rangers had appeared by this time and, warning camera-toting people like me to stay back, they pursued the bear, firing several shots into the air.

The young bear looked very frightened and swiftly scampered off into the forest to the left of the hotel. A hiker who was innocently approaching along the lakeside trail wisely followed the rangers' shouted advice, and stepped off the trail into the lake to let the speeding bear past.

It was an exciting introduction to the wildlife of Glacier National Park – which, with the adjoining Waterton Lakes National Park in British Columbia, Canada, forms the unique Waterton-Glacier International Peace Park, created in 1932.

Later, we travelled south to experience the legendary Going-to-the-Sun Road, which winds for 50 miles across the Continental Divide from St Mary Lake to Lake McDonald. Claimed to be one of the most scenic highways in the world, the road was built between 1911 and 1933 and was the brainchild of the first superintendent of Glacier National Park, Major William A Logan.

Mosaic of cobbles, McDonald Creek

St Mary Lake is the beautiful introduction to the Going-to-the-Sun Road for travellers coming from the east. This 10-mile-long, 300-foot-deep, glacier-carved lake is blessed with the most transparent, crystal-clear water, revealing a mosaic of smooth, water-worn pebbles exhibiting every color under the sun. Tiny, tree-studded Wild Goose Island provides the perfect foreground to the Amphitheater and Triple Divide Peaks which buttress its southern shores.

The climb towards the 6646-foot summit of Logan Pass (called after that first superintendent) passes directly under the Going-to-the-Sun Mountain, with views south towards the 9125-ft Reynolds Mountain, the shrinking Jackson and Blackfoot Glaciers, and 10,052-ft Mt Jackson.

The pull-out at Logan Pass may be the most spectacular one in the entire US national parks system, and is a must for most visitors.

81

Surrounded by towering peaks and the sweeping precipice of the Garden Wall, it is set in glorious wildflower meadows of glacier lilies, paintbrush and lupines.

A ranger explained how global warming was affecting the park. 'In 1850, the park had 150 glaciers' he said. 'Today, only 25 functional ones remain, and the predictions are that by 2030, most will have vanished.' The long descent to Lake McDonald passes directly under the Garden Wall and enters the switchback known as The Loop via the Triple Arches bridge buttresses. The bench carved out of the Garden Wall to carry The Loop is perhaps the greatest of many feats of engineering needed to build the road. Passing through the unlined 192-foot West Side Tunnel, eventually we reached the Avalanche Creek pull-out, with its breathtaking views of Heaven Peak (8987 ft) and the McDonald Creek valley. Leaving the mountains behind, we were soon at placid Lake McDonald and our overnight accommodation in an idyllic log cabin on the peaceful lake shore at rustic Lake McDonald Lodge.

A couple of years earlier, I had discovered that the Waterton-Glacier National Park is equally impressive from the Canadian side when I took the two-hour boat trip in the *MV International* from Waterton, Alberta. Passing down the mountain-rimmed length of Upper Waterton Lake, we crossed the 49th parallel for our prescribed half-hour stop in the US at Goat Haunt, Montana, one of the park's most remote locations. Any longer than that, we were told by a gun-toting ranger, and we would have to clear customs.

Beargrass on the Garden Wall, and Mt Reynolds

Yellowstone National Park

With a soft, swishing sound like that of rushing surf, Old Faithful dutifully threw up its 100-foot cascade of scalding water ...

Old Faithful at dawn

83

Nature, red in tooth and claw

'Buffalo jams' are quite common in the world's first national park at Yellowstone, which straddles the borders of Wyoming and Montana. Although the park service discourages drivers from stopping on the road to view wild animals, it still happens whenever a bear or one of the park's 5000-strong bison herd approaches.

So, on an early 'Wake up to Wildlife' tour, approaching the Tower-Roosevelt junction on the Canyon Village-Mammoth Hot Springs road, we were not surprised to see a queue of cars in front of us, with people clambering onto roofs with their cameras, binoculars and tripods.

Getting closer we could just see the head of a large black bear bobbing above the blue-gray sagebrush bushes. Then we noticed a mule deer doe anxiously circling the bear, not daring to approach. The manager of the Roosevelt Lodge cabins later told us the harrowing story: the bear had just taken the mule deer's fawn, and the crowd was watching as it tucked in to its venison breakfast.

This unexpected demonstration of Tennyson's 'Nature, red in tooth and claw' captured the essence of Yellowstone. It was a scene that could have been witnessed at any time since the Washburn-Langford-Doane expedition of 1870 finally proved to a disbelieving nation that the wonders of Yellowstone, as described by buckskin-clad backwoodsmen like John Colter and Jim Bridger, actually existed.

No one believed Bridger when he said the rivers in Yellowstone ran so fast that their

Minerva Terrace, Mammoth Hot Springs

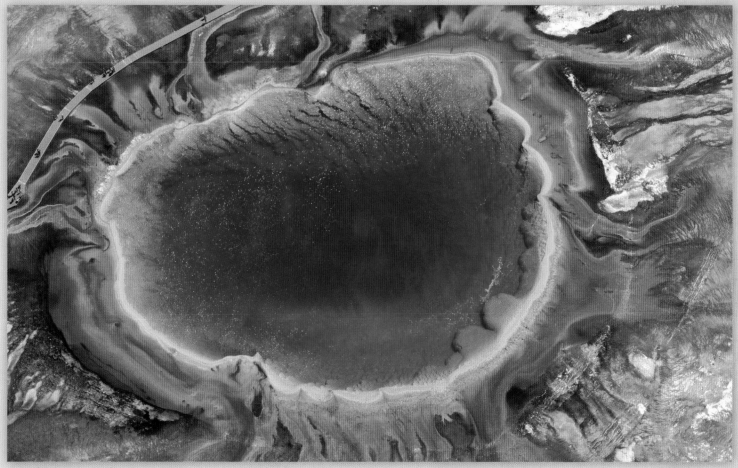

Grand Prismatic Pool

water steamed, or that you could catch a trout, throw it over your shoulder into a hot pool, and have it cooked for dinner.

The fact was, as Washburn reported to Congress, Bridger's tall tales were virtually all true. The 3450-square-mile Yellowstone National Park, designated by President Ulysses S Grant in 1872, contains half the world's geothermal features, and its 300 geysers make up two-thirds of the world's total.

We stayed for a couple of nights in the comfortably-rustic 'parkitecture' of Robert Reamer's Old Faithful Inn, which has kept watch over the world's most famous natural fountain for over a century. We were fortunate because our bedroom faced the geyser, and its regular eruptions marked off the hours as we tried to sleep.

With a soft, swishing sound like that of rushing surf, Old Faithful dutifully threw up its 100-foot cascade of scalding water

into the night sky, obscuring for a moment the myriad of twinkling stars. I got up at dawn to see the cascade transformed by the rising sun into a shimmering curtain of silver droplets.

Strolls from the busy Old Faithful area took us on wooden boardwalks through the thermal areas of Geyser Hill to the monumental Castle Geyser and Grand Giant, and eventually to the awesome, multi-colored void of Morning Glory Pool.

As we strode along the boardwalk on our way back to the inn we noticed a trembling beneath our feet, and much to our surprise and excitement – and to that of the regular 'geyser gazers' – the infrequent Beehive Geyser erupted in a graceful fountain right in front of us.

But there is much more to see in Yellowstone than the geysers. Popular sights include the dripping, snow-white and yellow travertine terraces of Mammoth Hot Springs, where we stayed in the former barracks of the 'Buffalo Soldiers', the units of the US Cavalry that once administered the park. We picnicked on the shores of the 136-square-mile vast expanse of Yellowstone Lake. At 7732 feet above sea level, it's America's largest high-altitude stretch of open water.

My one disappointment was that I didn't see any of Yellowstone's famous packs of re-introduced wolves, which have successfully restored the ecosystems and balance of nature in the Park.

But probably my favorite sight in Yellowstone is the Upper and Lower Falls of the Grand Canyon of the Yellowstone, close to Canyon Village. It's as spectacular in its own way as its better-known Arizona namesake and, for most tourists, easier to access.

And it was English-born artist Thomas Moran's panoramic painting of the Lower Falls, made after his appointment as artist to the Hayden Geological Survey of 1871, which proved to be crucial in persuading Congress to designate Yellowstone the world's first national park.

Dawn over Lower Yellowstone Falls

Yosemite National Park

The setting sun transformed Half Dome's massive west face into a shield of burnished gold.

Sunset over Half Dome, with twisted juniper

A temple to nature

My first impression of Yosemite was formed by Ansel Adams' masterful, subtly-graded monochrome portraits of its soaring granite walls. At the time I was working for England's Peak District National Park, and I never expected to see it myself. I read avidly John Muir's description of the Yosemite valley – which he did so much to protect, and where he lived and worked for about a decade. Yosemite, he wrote, was 'by far the grandest of all the special temples of Nature I was ever permitted to enter'.

Eventually, in 2001, I got my entry permit in the slightly surreal aftermath of the 9/11 attack. It was a life-changing moment. My wife Val and our friends realized how much this first visit meant to me; so when, on a glorious September afternoon, we arrived at Inspiration Point, they let me stand alone for a few minutes to take in the view.

And what a view! The landscape of my dreams was laid out before my unbelieving, tear-filled eyes. To the left, the great granite monolith of El Capitan soared 3000 feet from the valley floor in one breathtaking vertical leap, while on the opposite side of the valley the stepped profile of Cathedral Spires formed a clerical gray backdrop to the delicate, lacy spray of the Bridalveil Fall. Further up the valley, the unmistakeable monk's cowl of Half Dome kept a stony and silent watch.

Muir's theory of the glacial genesis of the valley was controversial when he first expressed it. To me, it all seemed

El Capitan

patently obvious. Next morning, I saw the shifting, diaphanous dawn mist fill the valley, just as the Ice Age glaciers had done some 10,000 years ago, patiently but inexorably carving it out.

We stayed in the 1930s log cabins of Curry Village, tucked beneath the beetling, skyscraper walls of Glacier Point. Having chased out a few unwelcome 'critters' from our cabins, on that magical, balmy first evening we had dinner alfresco. The setting sun transformed Half Dome's massive west face into a shield of burnished gold. I felt as if I'd died and gone to heaven …

After a night disturbed only by the sound of enterprising black bears attacking the waste bins, I rose early and walked down to the mist-shrouded Merced River. As the mist slowly cleared, flocks of red-winged blackbirds and iridescent blue-winged Steller's jays quarrelled noisily in the bone-white skeletons of fallen trees. Across the river, the stony face of Half Dome and the Royal Arches gradually emerged.

Later, we travelled up the Big Oak Flat Road to reach the beautiful, flower-decked Alpine pastures of Toulumne Meadows. Wandering through knee-high stands of Jeffrey shooting stars, scarlet paintbrushes and bright yellow monkeyflowers, we reached the steep scramble up the smooth slick-rock, eroded slopes of Lambert Dome, and an amazing view across the granite domes of the upper valley.

On later visits, I explored the valley more thoroughly, taking several well-marked trails around the valley. I enjoyed grandstand views of the valley from the thigh-burning four-mile trail from Glacier Point down to the valley floor. We enjoyed a cup of tea in the Ahwahnee Hotel, named after this valley which is known to the

Vernal Fall, Merced River

89

indigenous Ahwahneechee Indians as 'Ahwahnee' – meaning 'valley that looks like a gaping mouth'. And that evening I enjoyed actor Lee Stetson's performance as 'John Muir Live' in the Yosemite Theater.

On another occasion, we rose early before the crowds of visitors' cars had choked the inadequate one-way traffic system. We walked to the foot of the twin Yosemite Falls – at a combined height of 2425 feet, some of the highest in the States – and witnessed beautifully translucent rainbows in the dancing, shifting spray. Muir had described the 1430-foot upper fall as 'a snowy, chanting throng of comet-like streamers' after he had boldly shuffled along a three-inch ledge towards the very lip of the falls for a closer view.

My favorite Yosemite trail is the six-mile Vernal Fall-Nevada Fall Loop from the Happy Isles campsite. On a blisteringly hot ascent of the Mist Trail, I was mercifully cooled by spray from the 317-foot thunderous Vernal Fall. I returned by a switchback of the John Muir Trail, with fine views of the bald granite knob of Liberty Cap and the 594-foot cascade of the Nevada Fall, the broad-topped Mt Broderick, and the batholith of Half Dome from a different angle.

Yosemite will always hold a very special place in my heart. This magnificent natural temple to Nature has captivated many millions of visitors since John Muir first wrote about its beauties, and part of me lingers there still.

Half Dome, Liberty Cap and Nevada Fall

'There is an elegance to their forms which stirs the imagination with a singular power ...'

Clarence E Dutton

Zion National Park

Towers of the Virgin

Heaven on earth

As we set out from Springdale, dawn was bathing the spires of the West Temple, The Sentinel and the Towers of the Virgin in a golden, glowing light. It augured well for a day when we were going to explore the inner sanctuaries of Zion, the 15-mile-long, half-mile-deep canyon cut into the Kayenta and Navajo sandstones of the Colorado Plateau.

Formed over millions of years by the uplift of the surrounding plateau, aided by the tremendous erosive power of the North Fork of the Virgin River, Zion Canyon was named by the first Mormon settler, Isaac Behunin in the mid-19th century. It was the nearest thing to heaven that he had seen, so he named it after the city of his God.

The exalted names given to the golden, red and white sandstone walls and bristling peaks reflect the reverential awe in which they were held by those first visitors: East and West Temples, Great White Throne, Altar of Sacrifice, Court of the Patriarchs, Organ, Pulpit and the vertiginous viewpoint of Angel's Landing.

The latter, a 5790-foot-high spur which hangs over the Upper Canyon, was given its celestial name by a Methodist minister, the Rev Frederick Vining Fisher on a day trip in 1916, after one of his companions had commented: 'only an angel could land on it'.

Angel's Landing on the north western rim of the canyon was our destination, and we set off from the site of Behunin's log cabin at Zion Lodge along the river to The Grotto, and over the sturdy metal footbridge across the rushing waters of the Virgin River.

Virgin River Narrows

The West Rim Trail climbed gently through the cottonwoods, with impressive views of the towering 6744-ft-monolith of The Great White Throne (also named by Fisher) on the opposite wall, and the winding course of the Big Bend in the Virgin River below.

The trail now steepened between the steep, overhanging walls of the appropriately-chilly Refrigerator Canyon to reach the 21 symmetrical, 60° switchbacks affectionately known as Walter's Wriggles. This magnificent piece of footpath engineering was named after former park superintendent Walter Ruesch, who oversaw its construction in 1924.

Reaching the junction of trails at Scout's Landing, some of us were relieved to find that the east fork to Angel's Landing was closed due to rockfalls. The park literature warned that this 'strenuous' knife-edge ridge had long drop-offs, and should not be attempted by anyone fearful of heights. The warning sign provided confirmation, welcome to some, that we could go no further.

But the views from Scout's Landing were reward enough, extending down on the dramatic fin known as The Organ and across to winding Echo Canyon to the north and over the awesome void to the white-capped Great White Throne.

The Great White Throne, perhaps Zion's most impressive and photographed monolith, provides an instant geology lesson about the sedimentary nature of the Zion's sandstones. Topped by a

Weeping Rock Pool, Great White Throne

vertical wall of vivid white rock created from an oxide-reduced Navajo sandstone called limonite, it dominates the upper canyon. Below the shining band of white, bands of rust-red Navajo and Kayenta sandstones are streaked with black oxide stains known as desert varnish, carved into a fantastic array of alcoves, arches, towers and hoodoos.

Descending the way we had come, we had time to explore both the Lower and Middle Emerald Pools, where twin waterfalls and hanging gardens of moss and lichens mark the spring line in the impervious sandstone. Tufa rock had formed in the calcium-rich limestone of the tranquil pools beneath.

At the head of the canyon, just beyond the Temple of Sinawava turn-out (named after the coyote god of the Paiutes), the valley narrows to a claustrophobic 20-foot-wide gorge. The walls on either side rise to 2000 feet above the river. The traverse of The Narrows is one of the most strenuous, 16-mile off-trail hikes in the park because it involves wading through the river which is subject to sudden flash floods.

In summer, a free shuttle bus service takes you the six miles from Springdale to the Temple of Sinawava, and private vehicles are not allowed. This practical use of public transport has saved Zion from being potentially choked by visitor traffic, the fate of some popular US national parks. Maybe Zion's vision suggests a way of reducing environmental impact while still providing easy access to some of the finest landscapes in *Wild America*.

94

Fall at the Temple of Sinawava

Find your park

To mark the 2016 centennial of its 'Organic Act', the National Park Service has set a goal 'to connect with and create the next generation of park visitors, supporters and advocates'. Its *Find your park* public awareness campaign was spearheaded by Michelle Obama and Laura Bush.

'It may be a place, a feeling, a state of mind' the campaign suggests, 'so get up, get out there, and find your park'. David and I hope that in a modest way this book will help you to go out and find your park; you may discover, as did John Muir, that by going out for a walk, he was really going in.

Biographies

David Muench

David Muench has spent the last 50 years photographing America's National Parks and other wilderness areas. He is the primary photographer of over 50 books and his work appears in many magazines, posters and private collections. His website is listed below.

Roly Smith

Roly Smith is a freelance writer, editor and media consultant, and the author of over 80 books on walking and the countryside. He was chairman of the British Outdoor Writers' and Photographers' Guild (1990-2001), president (2001-13) and is now its vice-president.

National Park Service

The National Park Service website is at *www.nps.gov* and there's a separate website for its centennial campaign: *www.findyourpark.com*.

Photo credits

All photographs are © copyright David Muench 1953-2014 *www.davidmuenchphotography.com* except for page 4 © 1984 Muir-Hanna Trust/Holt-Atherton Special Collections, and (David Muench photo above) Walter Reichart. The outline map of the US used to indicate locations throughout is courtesy of *FreeVectorMaps.com*.

Acknowledgements

I owe great thanks to my wife, Ruth Rudner, for sharing her knowledge of America's wildland. And thanks to my daughter Zandria Beraldo, son Marc Muench, and my assistant, Page Morgan, for helping to put all the pieces together.

David Muench

I'd like to thank my loving wife Val and our children Claire, Neil and Iain, for allowing me to pursue my dreams. Sincere thanks go to our good American friends Gene and Sylvia Tester of East Dundee, Illinois; Homer and Deanna Chappell of Portland, Oregon and Jim and the late Larraine Crow of Pacifica, California for being generous and genial guides to many of the places featured in this book.

I also want to record my heartfelt gratitude to David Muench, in my opinion the greatest living photographer of Wild America, for so readily agreeing to be my partner in this book. It's been a real privilege to work with him.

Roly Smith

The publisher thanks Ruth Rudner for the valuable comments she made on the draft version, and Lindsay Merriman for proofreading.

Rucksack Readers

Rucksack Readers, a publisher of outdoor books, specialises in weatherproof guidebooks to adventurous walks worldwide. Visit *www.rucsacs.com* and *www.rucsacs.com/books/wam*.

Index